The Amazing Adventure of

Dan

the

Pawn

Simon Garrow

'Wakey, wakey!' The cry echoed around and faded into silence.

Then slowly, one by one, little white heads appeared out of the box. The Pawns rubbed their sleepy eyes, yawned and stretched, as they stumbled over the black and white squares to their places on the second row.

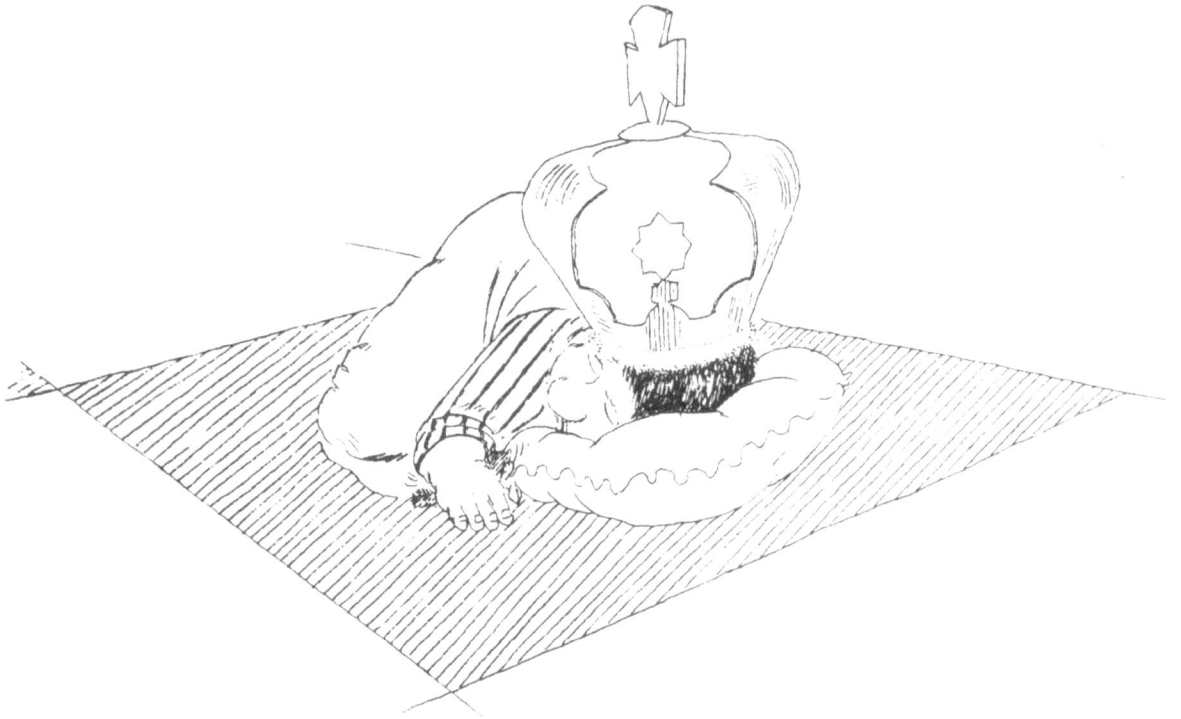

The sun was not yet up, so the gloom obscured a large round figure lying in the middle of the back row. It was the King. He had been too lazy to go back to the box and had slept there all night.

Suddenly he snored, startling a nearby Pawn, who jumped with a scream. The King opened an eye and stared at the little Pawn.

Then he grunted:

'You're new!'

'Y-yes, Your Majesty,' stammered the Pawn, 'I'm a replacement.'

'A replacement! — why?' said the King.

'The Queen's Pawn got lost, Your Majesty — I've been called in at the last minute.'

'Do you know the rules?' asked the King.

'N-no, Your Majesty.' The new Pawn felt foolish enough already not knowing whether to bow or not. He was awkward in his strange white uniform, and he was afraid that the great heavy helmet he was wearing would topple him over if he tried anything like bowing.

'Well, get my Pawn to show you round....' The King's eye closed and he began to snore again.

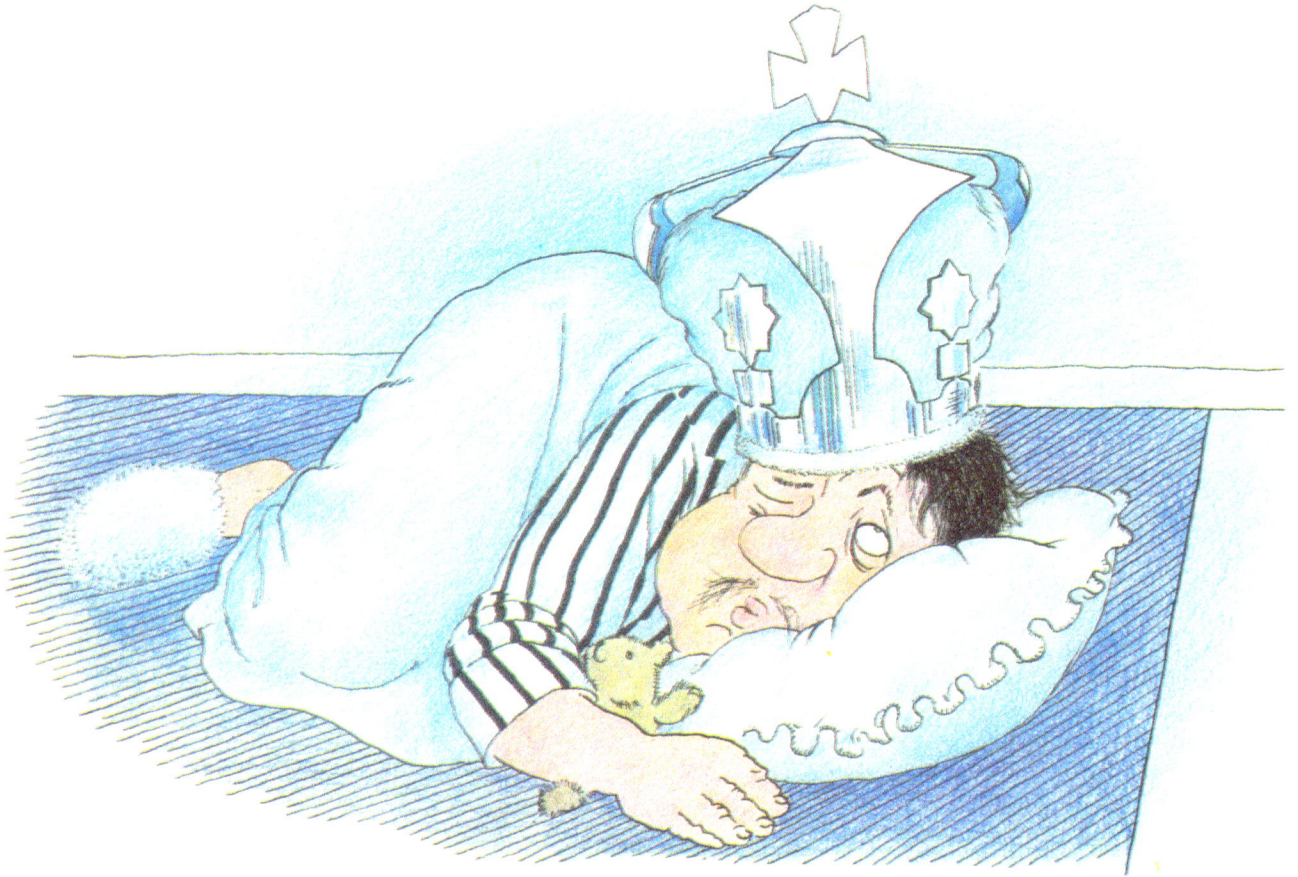

The little Pawn peered about him: all the soldiers looked the same to him. But a Pawn who had been standing near held out his hand, and, smiling, said:

'Hello, I'm Ernie, the King's Pawn. What's your name?'

'Dan,' said the newcomer shyly, and shook Ernie's hand.

'Welcome Dan, now let me explain what's going on. We are part of an army that is soon going to fight to capture the enemy King.'

He pointed across the battlefield to where the black army could be made out in the dawn twilight, preparing itself for battle.

'And that army will attack us, to try to capture our King. I'd better let you know what we Pawns do; there's no need to worry about the others.'

'Others?' thought Dan. He looked around: there was no one but the sleeping King, everyone else was a Pawn. However Ernie was continuing:

'Pawns march only forwards — that means no side-stepping and no coming back.

'If you want to fight, you may attack anyone in front of you who dares stand on a square the same colour as yours. Supposing you're on a white square, you can attack anybody on either of the white squares just ahead of you; or if you're on a black square, you can attack anybody on either of the black squares just ahead of you.'

'So we march forwards — but fight diagonally,' said Dan, trying to impress.

He looked down to see what colour square he was on, but immediately flipped head over heels and found himself ignominiously on his back.

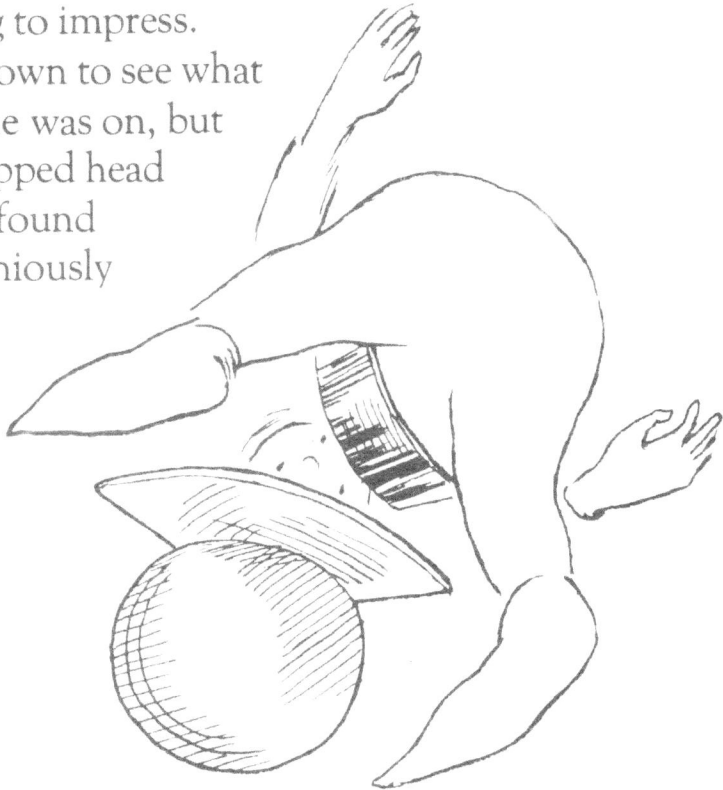

'Careful!' Ernie was chuckling as he helped Dan
to his feet, 'these helmets are quite heavy. I was
always falling over at first, it takes some time to get
used to them, even then you can't exactly dash
around. Remember, we march or fight only one
square at a time, though on his first move, while still
full of energy, every Pawn can march over two
squares if necessary. Here, have a sandwich? Egg and
relish.'

Dan gratefully took one and stretched. He hadn't slept at all well that night; he'd been so nervous and quite unused to the crowded conditions.

'By the way', he said, 'somewhere below me last night there was a talkative Pawn who kept everyone awake, boasting about having just "Queened" or "done the eights". What was he going on about?'

'Oh that was Hugh, he'd just done it', said Ernie, trying to keep the envy out of his voice. 'Any Pawn who reaches the eighth square can change into any other piece, even a Queen.'

Dan frowned, it was difficult enough understanding the importance of being a Queen's Pawn, let alone trying to imagine what the Queen herself should feel like.

'Tell me about the Queen', he said.

'Some people find her rather frightening, but I've got a lot of admiration for her. I've been close to the King for too long. He's really lazy. But the Queen has so much energy. She can organise Pawns, stop the Bishops squabbling, do the housework and then rush right over the battlefield in any direction she wants.'

While Ernie was talking, Dan's attention was drawn to an odd creaking noise behind them. Two enormous castles had appeared and were now standing solidly and silently in the two corners of the battlefield. Dan caught sight of them and pointed excitedly:

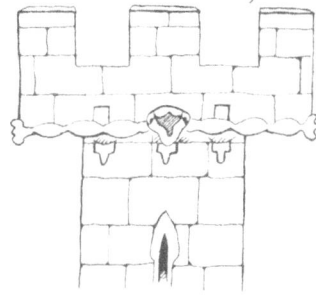

'Look!'

Ernie turned and smiled.

'They make the most valuable fighting force we have', he said proudly, then added looking nervously round, 'of course, apart from the Queen'.

'Can we go and have a closer look?' asked Dan eagerly.

Ernie frowned at him with disapproval; obviously Pawns didn't do that sort of thing. But it was lost on Dan who had already set off towards the edge of the field and Ernie had to hurry to catch up with him.

The other Pawns were busy polishing armour and sharpening swords. They stared disdainfully at the two as they passed, making Dan feel very small, though, naturally, he was the same size as every one of them.

Ernie and Dan arrived puffing at the foot of the castle, whose battlements blazed red with the morning sun. They could now hear faint whirrings and hisses coming from inside the walls, but the castle remained motionless.

It was not as big as Dan had at first thought, but he said:

'Looks as solid as a rock!'

'Oh I don't know about that', said Ernie (any grumpiness had now quite evaporated), 'it makes a great creaking noise when it moves. For some reason we nickname it 'Rook'. Imitating the castle, he lurched about, giving as long and as fierce a croak as his throat would allow.

'R-r-r-r-r-r-ooooooooo...K!' He stopped abruptly, coughing and giggling. 'They tear across the battleground like steam engines and go as fast backwards or sideways as well!'

'I feel very protected standing next to it', said Dan.

All of a sudden they heard a sharp clattering of hooves.

Both Pawns turned to see an armoured Knight on a powerful white horse come prancing over the field in strange angled leaps. Jumping this way, then that, with a great deal of creaking and clanking the fierce horse and rider pounded gradually closer.

Dan was sure he would be trampled on and, terrified, he scrambled closer to the castle.

The noise grew and grew. Dan shut his eyes, but at the last second the Knight changed direction and, in a cloud of dust, landed on the square next to him.

'Frightened of your own Knights!' jeered the Knight, looking down at Dan and breaking into a frenzied, whinnying cackle.

The other Pawns began to join in, sniggering and pointing.

'Do you think he'll do the eights with nerves like that!'

'What a wet!'

The Knight then turned to them and roared:

'Which of you scum has pinched my polish?'

Ernie put his hand on Dan's shoulder,

I'd better explain. Knights always think they fool the enemy by pretending to go one way and then suddenly changing direction and going another — two squares here, then one square there. But there's no surprise, as they do it every time.'

Just then, another Knight came onto the field and moved exactly as he had predicted. One jump, two, then a jump to the side. One, two, one to the side.

'Arrogant brutes!' Ernie bit crossly into an egg sandwich.

'Just because they can jump and no one else can. Knights are such bullies sometimes. That one who frightened you just now will be really pleased: he hasn't had a reaction like that for a long time. If you ask me, I think they're upset at being tethered out by the castles. But, as everyone knows, the Queen can't stand the smell of horses.'

Dan fully agreed with the Queen's taste; the wild-eyed, snorting horse with its whisking tail and heavy hooves was keeping his nerves quite on edge.

'Shall we go back?' he said to Ernie.

Just then from the other side of the field, they heard a cheer.

The Pawns were crying out:

'The Queen's coming, the Queen's coming!'

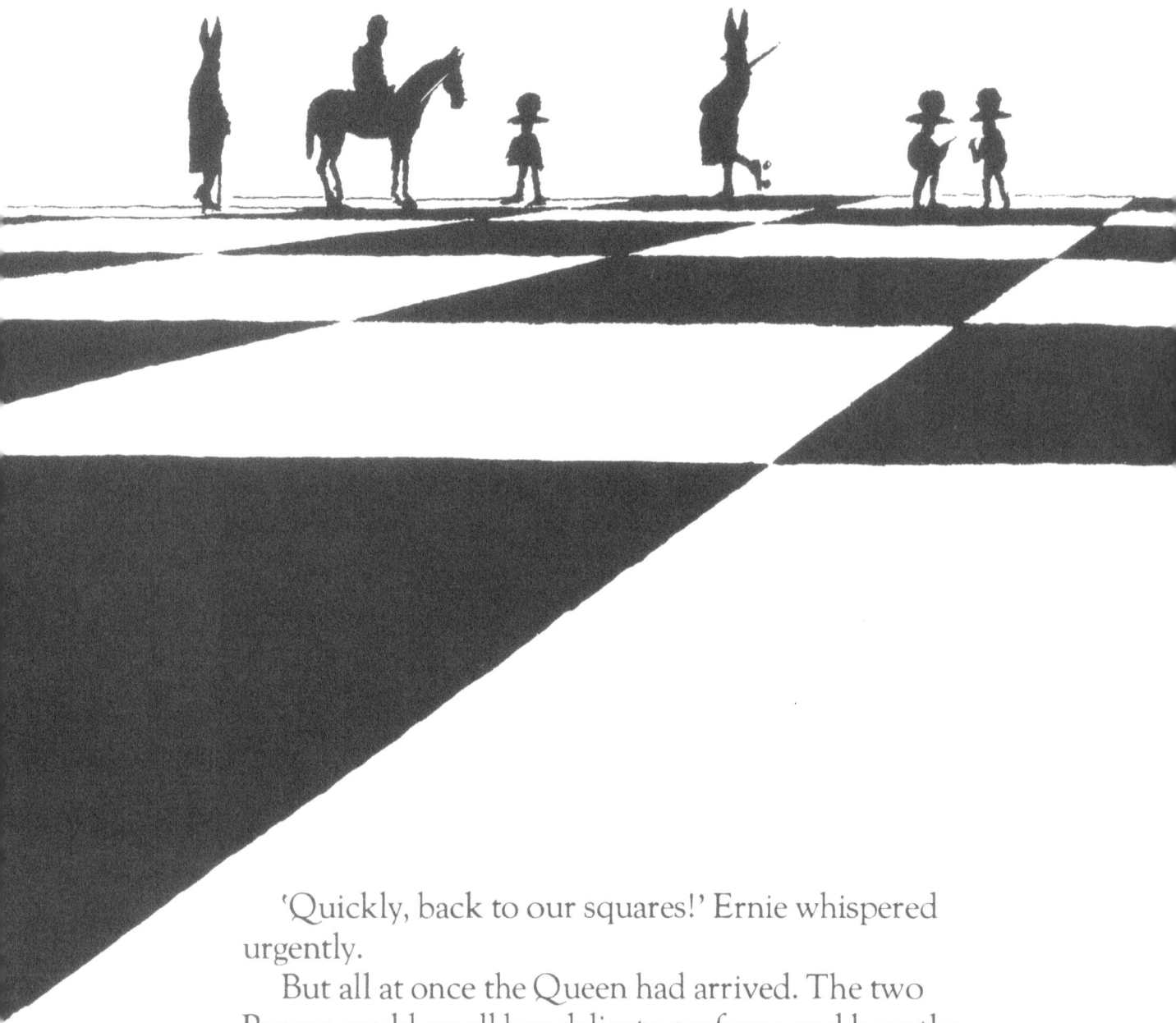

'Quickly, back to our squares!' Ernie whispered urgently.

But all at once the Queen had arrived. The two Pawns could smell her delicate perfume and hear the crisp rustle of her starched white dress. She was glaring up and down the ranks, checking that everyone was in position.

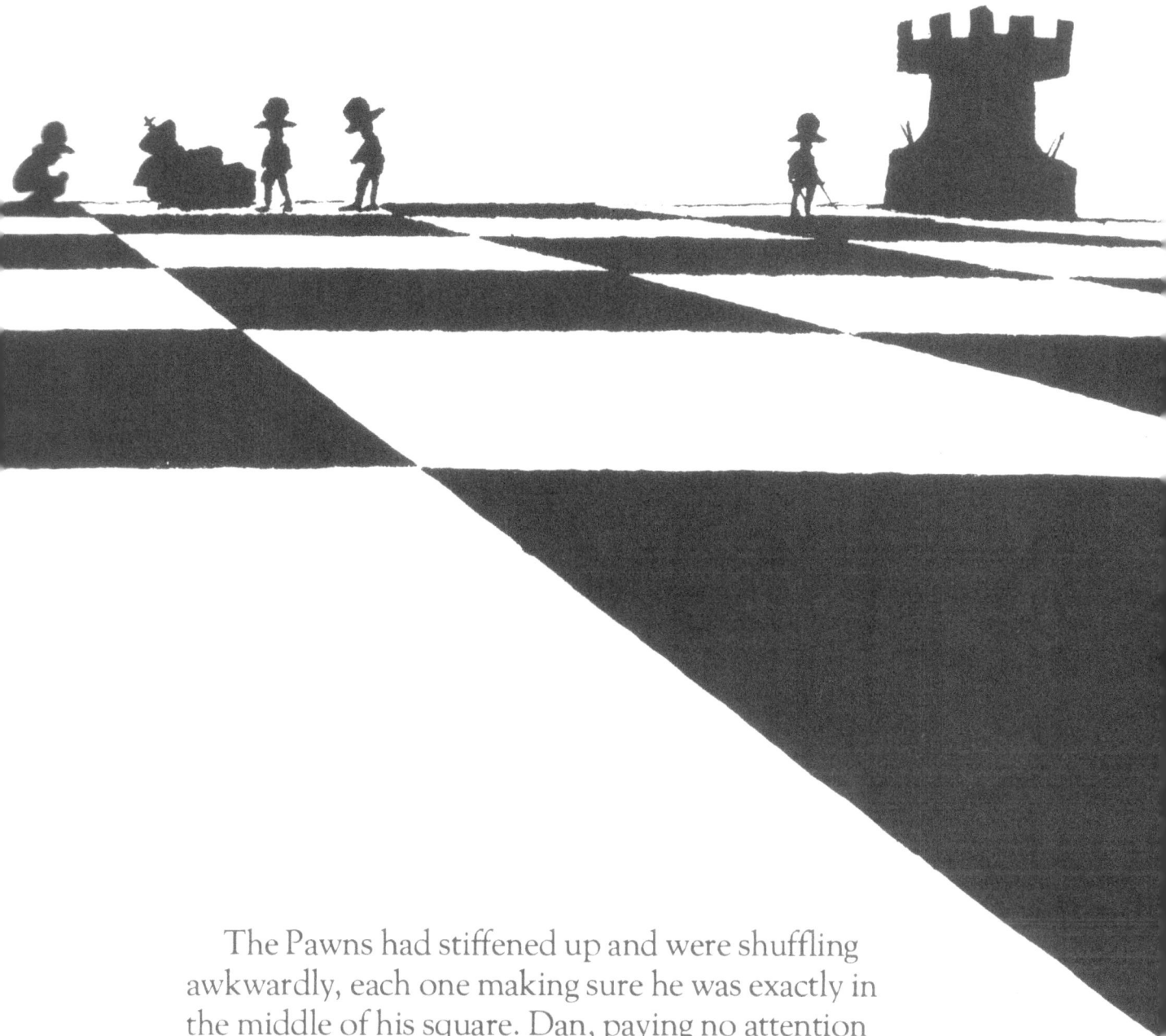

The Pawns had stiffened up and were shuffling awkwardly, each one making sure he was exactly in the middle of his square. Dan, paying no attention to them, was staring at his Queen, and probably would have stared all morning, but the Bishops arrived immediately.

21

'Make way on the white squares, I come to protect Her Royal Majesty the Queen!' The imperious voice rang out as a Bishop flashed over the white squares and halted with a flourish on the square where Ernie should have been.

'Make way on the black squares, I come to protect Her Royal Majesty the Queen!' A second Bishop sped over the black squares, straight over the square that Dan should have been on.

'As you see, Your Majesty, I arrived first', the panting Bishop on Ernie's square bowed low and obsequiously.

'My dear chap', the other Bishop managed to snort, 'you are on the white squares and therefore the King's Bishop, kindly leave the attendance of Her Majesty to me!'

He tried to catch the Queen's eye, as he too bowed towards her. But the Queen had started on her early morning exercises and it was no use trying

to win her attention. The first Bishop slunk off to his square beside the sleeping King. Ernie and Dan managed to sneak back to their correct places.

'They're always quarrelling', whispered Ernie. 'To keep them separate, the Queen gives one the run of the black squares, and the other the run of the white. She must be quite fond of them as she uses them a lot.'

Dan could hear that the Queen had finished her exercises.

He was just about to turn around and introduce himself to her, but a sharp tut-tutting and a violent shake of the head from Ernie stopped him; obviously Pawns did not talk to Queens. But, Dan worried, supposing she talked to him, it would be awful to be tongue tied. He prepared a polite inquiry about her binoculars just in case, and stared out in front of him.

Then he noticed the enemy. The sun had risen higher in the sky. Squinting out across the chequered battlefield, Dan felt a quick thrill of terror running through his entire body, as he saw clearly the black army motionless and ready to fight.

Exhausted and sticky after his expedition with Ernie, Dan stood still and waited. Now the whole white army was ready; everyone was looking out across the field at the enemy lines, not a thing moved.

All of a sudden the quiet was broken by a command from the white Queen:

'My Pawn....' Dan froze, he couldn't believe it, but he knew Ernie was looking at him. '...forward two squares!'

1 Pawn – d4

Dan now felt awful. His mouth was dry, the smell of horses and perfume made him feel sick, his legs were wobbly, he thought he was going to faint. But hardly knowing what he was doing, Dan found his legs carrying him forward, first on to a white square and then on to a black square again.

He was now standing right out in front of the row of Pawns, his heart pounding so loud that he was sure they could all hear it. Gradually he began to feel better as he realised he probably looked very brave.

It was black's turn, and the black King ordered his Bishop's Pawn forward. Dan turned to look at his army, wondering what the next move was going to be. The Queen was watching intently the black Pawn stepping out towards them, and she was whispering something to her Bishop.

When the black Pawn had stopped moving, the Bishop picked up his robes and sped over the black squares to within two squares of the enemy front line.

1   Pawn - f5

2 Bishop - g5

28

'What a nerve!' The shriek from the black Queen made Dan jump. Then he heard her order the Pawn in front of the castle to attack the Bishop.

2 Pawn – h6

The castle Pawn duly stepped forward on to a black square, and, pulling the ugliest face he could, shook his sword at the Bishop.

3 Bishop – h4

The Bishop merely stepped back one square. He was now by the edge of the battlefield.

'Chase him!' the black Queen yelled, and an eager little Pawn, who had been waiting in front of a snorting

3   Pawn – g5

horse, rushed forward growling, and in his turn shook his sword at the Bishop.

The Bishop pretended to yawn, put his nose in the air and stepped

4 Bishop – g3

back again one square. Dan now looked upon the Bishop as his hero.

'Marvellous!' he kept saying to himself, full of admiration.

The black Queen
was boiling with rage.
But there was a
certain note of
triumph in her
voice as she
ordered the
Bishop's Pawn to
attack. Then she
barked:
  'He's trapped!'
Dan stared and
held his breath.

4   Pawn – f4

The trapped white Bishop looked disdainfully down on the fierce little Pawn, then slowly turned and smiled at his Queen.

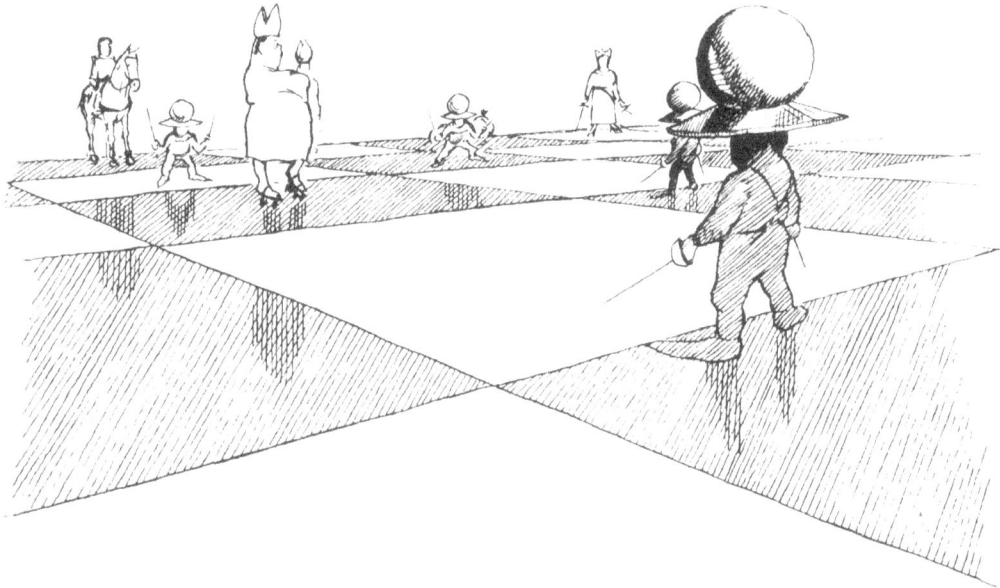

Dan saw her lean down and quietly ask Ernie to move on to a black square. (Now, Dan understood, if only the enemy would give her time — perhaps by taking the Bishop — the Queen could win the battle by running out on the white squares and calling 'Checkmate!' from the edge of the battlefield.)

5 Pawn – e3

But the black King had been watching what was going on and fully realised the terrible danger he was in. Where were his protective Pawns? He cursed his wife.

5   Pawn – h5

She ignored him,
but quickly ordered
the castle's Pawn to
step another square
forward. If the white
Queen now wanted
to call 'Check', she
would have to
capture this Pawn
first — and then the
castle would get her!

Then Dan heard his King's Bishop move out on to the white square just behind him. This really put the black King into a panic, he screamed at his wife: 'Now look what you've done! That other Bishop is going to get me, and I've got nowhere to hide!'

The horror of the situation began to dawn on the whole black army, and the Pawns started whispering nervously amongst themselves. The Queen's voice, when it sounded over the tense chatter, had an immediate calming effect.

6   Castle – h6

She efficiently commanded the castle to move forward to be ready to capture the Bishop should he dare call 'Check'.

Dan was looking at his Queen. She appeared very excited, her cheeks were tinged with red. Suddenly, with a loud war-cry she charged over to the edge of the field. Then having captured the Pawn, she glared down towards the enemy King and shouted:

7 Queen – h5
Check

'Check!'

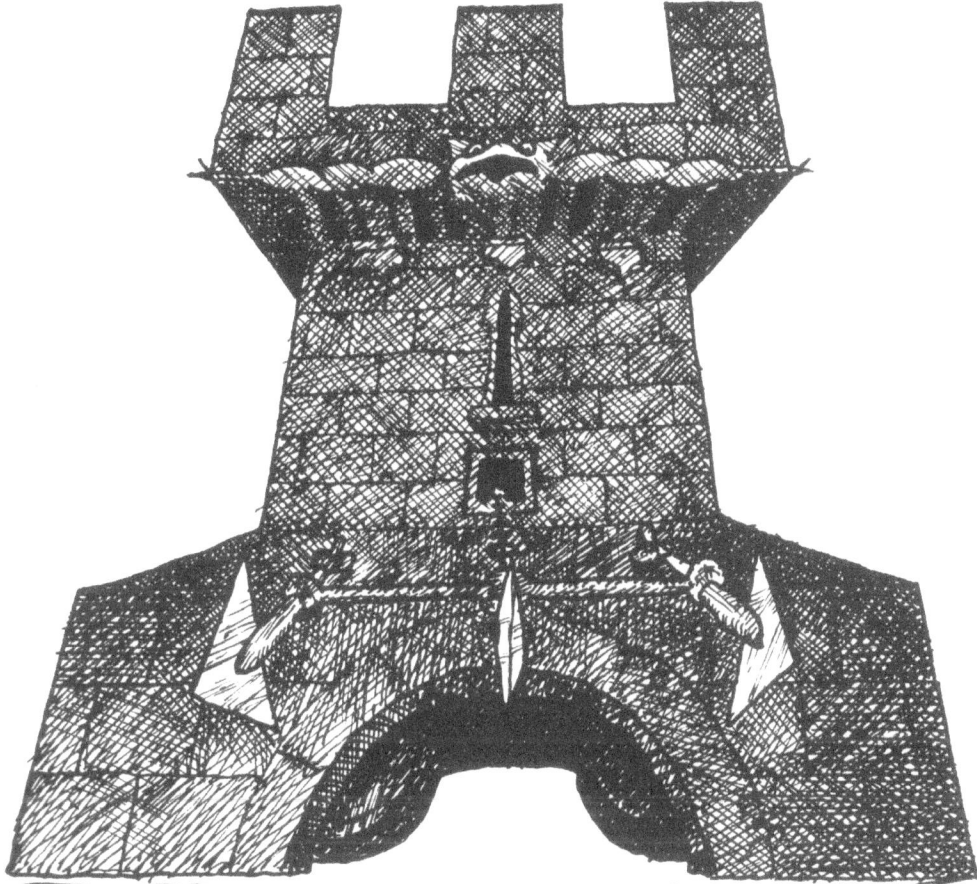

The black King nearly jumped out of his skin.
But in a flash his castle had creaked forward and
removed the Queen with no difficulty at all.

7   Castle (h5)
X Queen

There was a dreadful hush, as though people could not believe their eyes. Both armies stood utterly still, even the horses had stopped pawing the ground.

Dan's skin felt all prickly. His helmet was suddenly very heavy.

But then there was a busy rustling noise behind him; the Bishop was gathering up his robes, then he was off. He glided smoothly over the white squares like a great white bird, halted, pointed his sword at the black King and said:

8 Bishop – g6
Mate

'Check Mate!'

Immediately a loud cheer went up from the white army and the black King gave himself up. Bubbling with relief, everyone gathered round the Bishops to congratulate them (of course they were soon quarrelling about who had played the most important part). Dan and Ernie did a little jig.

'Well done. What did you think?' said Ernie.

'Fantastic!' said Dan.

Before long the Queen was striding on to the field and organising a party. By the time it came to go back it was late. Dan was happy though immensely tired. Gradually the only thing that occupied his mind was the thought of a long cosy sleep back in the box, where now, he felt, he really belonged.

The Rules of Chess

1 Make sure the board is the right way round (i.e. with a white square in the bottom right-hand corner).

2 Only one piece can occupy a square.

3 Any piece can take any piece, except the king cannot be taken.

4 No jumping (except knights).

5 The object is to capture the king.

6 When you threaten the king with a piece say 'check'.

7 The king must get out of check. You can take the attacker, shield the king by putting another piece in the way (impossible when the attacker is a knight) or move the king to a safe square. You cannot ignore check and move another piece. If you can't stop the check, the game is over and this is known as checkmate.

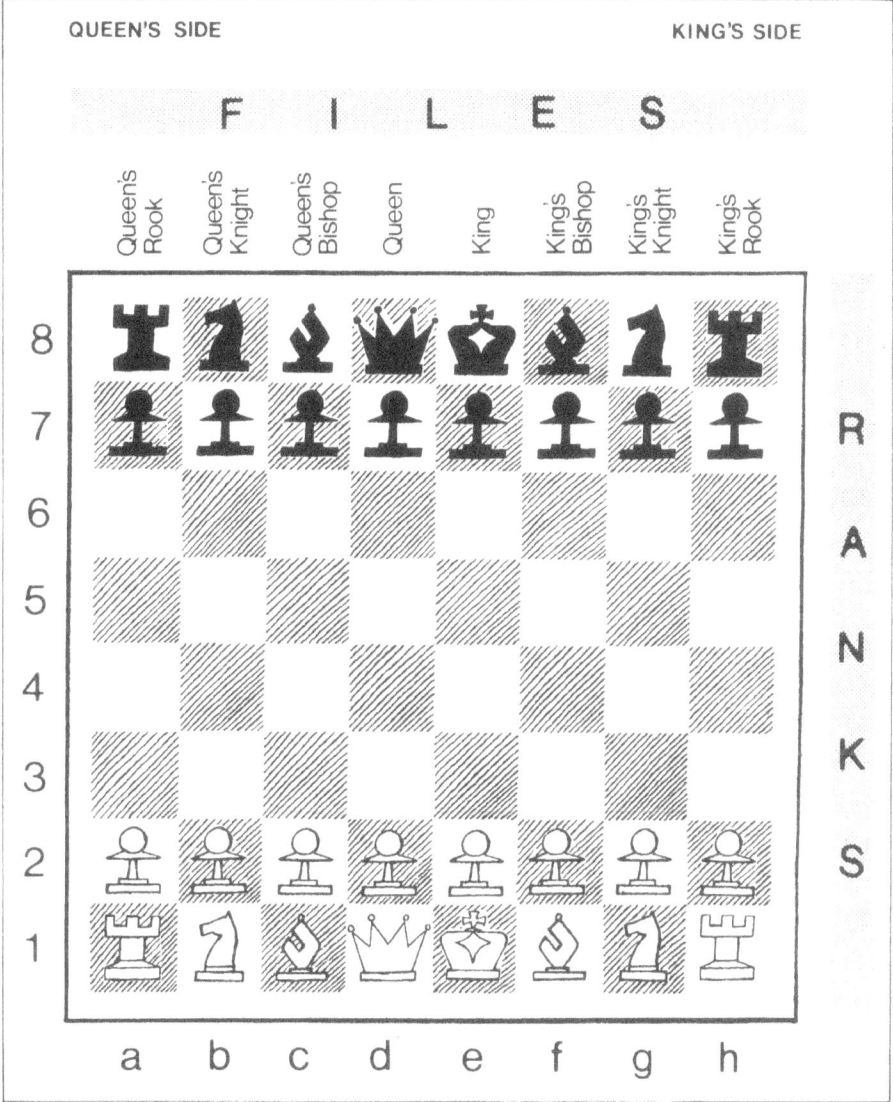

QUEEN'S SIDE   KING'S SIDE

F I L E S

Queen's Rook | Queen's Knight | Queen's Bishop | Queen | King | King's Bishop | King's Knight | King's Rook

R
A
N
K
S

8 7 6 5 4 3 2 1

a b c d e f g h

45

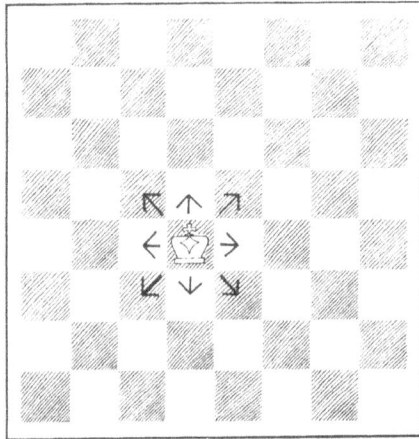

King – One square in any direction.

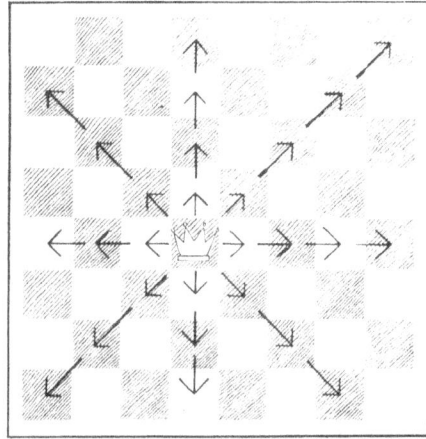

Queen – As far as she likes in a straight line in any direction.

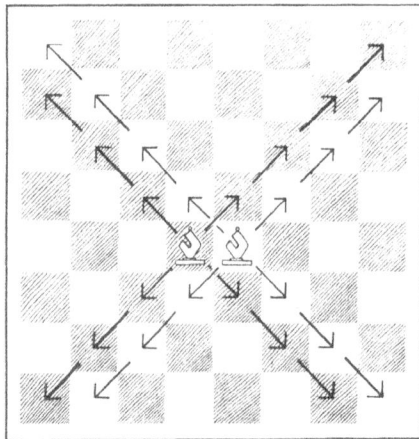

Bishop – As far as he likes in a straight line diagonally on whatever colour he is on.

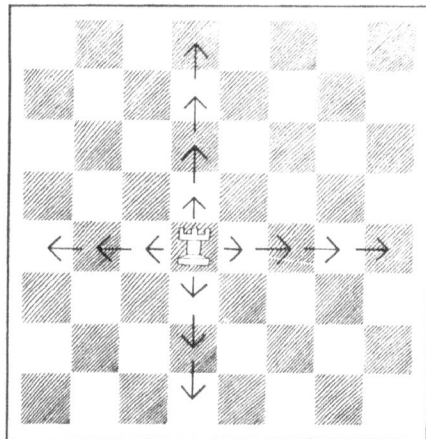

Castle (Rook) – As far as he likes in a straight line, forwards, backwards or sideways.

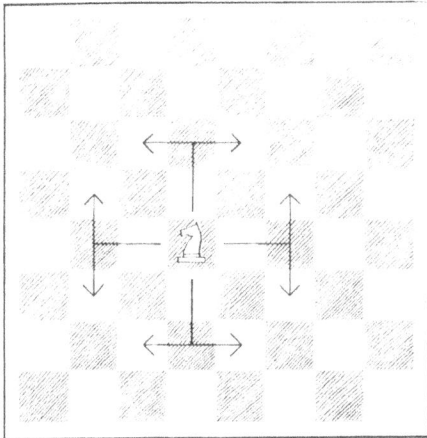

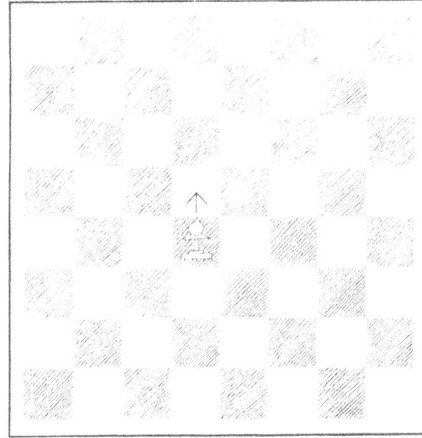

Knight – Jumps forwards, backwards or sideways two squares then one square at right angles. Only the square he wishes to land on need be clear or occupied by an enemy that he will take.

Pawn – One square forward (can move two, if desired, on his first go). But he takes one square diagonally.

9 When a pawn reaches the 8th rank it must be promoted, i.e. become a queen or knight or bishop or castle of its own colour. (It is possible to have two or more queens, though not two kings.)

10 'En passant'. A pawn A on the 5th rank can take (only on the next move) a pawn B who decides to come out two squares, thus putting himself on the same rank and next to A. A takes him as though B had only moved one square, so moves diagonally on to his 6th rank.

11 'Castling'. The king can do this with the queen's castle or his own castle, providing all the squares between them are empty. If neither the king nor the relevant castle has moved, the castle moves to the square next to the king and the king (in the same go) jumps over the castle on to the square on the other side. This cannot be done when you are in check, or if an enemy piece attacks the square through which the king has to pass.

12 'Stalemate'. This occurs if the king is not in check and he is the only piece who can move, and yet he can only move into check. Stalemate is a draw.

13 'Notation'.
King = K;   Queen = Q;   Castle (Rook) = R;   Bishop = B;
Knight = N;   Pawn = P;   Castling Kingside = 0 – 0;
Castling Queenside = 0 – 0 – 0;   takes = x;   En passant = e.p.;
Check = ch

14 White starts.

ISBN 978 1 908267 99 3

Artwork refreshed by Riva Productions Ltd
Published by AtoZeasy Learning(UK) Ltd
27 Old Gloucester St
London WC1N 3AX

www.ingramcontent.com/pod-product-compliance
Lightning Source LLC
LaVergne TN
LVHW072119070426

835511LV00002B/28